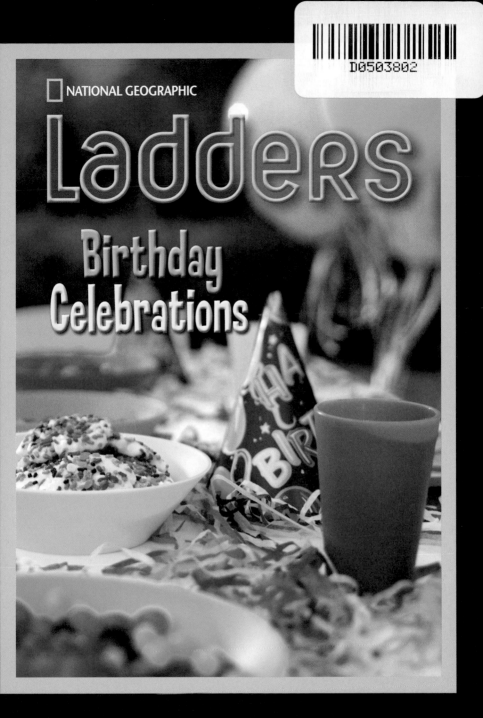

NATIONAL GEOGRAPHIC

Ladders

Birthday Celebrations

International

by Elizabeth Gilbert | illustrations by Leslie Harrington

"Happy Birthday!" Around the World

People around the world speak different languages. They say "Happy Birthday" in different ways. Here are some ways to say "Happy Birthday."

Happy Birthday
(HA-peeh BERTH-day)
English

Janmadin mubarak ho
(jahn-mah-DIN moo-BAH-rahk HOH)
Hindi

Alles gute zum Geburtstag
(AH-les goot zoom geh-BURS-tahg)
German

S'dniom roshedenea
(s dnyom rozh-DEE-nyah)
Russian

Birthday Bash

Feliz cumpleaños
(fay-LEES coom-plee-AHN-yohs)
Spanish

Maligayang kaarawan
(maah-lee-GAH-yang kah-AH-rah-wahn)
Tagalog

Kule sana wintie tayyiba (to a girl)
(koo-LEH SAH-na win-TEE tie-EE-bah)
Arabic (in Egypt)

Kule sana winta tayib (to a boy)
(koo-LEH SAH-na win-TAH TIE-eeb)
Arabic (in Egypt)

Otanjobi omedeto gozaimasu
(oh-tan-JOH-bee oh-med-ih-toh goh-zah-ee-mas)
Japanese

Feliz Aniversário
(fay-LEEZ ah-nee-vair-SAH-ree-yoh)
Portuguese

Sheng ri kuai le
(shung-rur KWAI-luh)
Mandarin

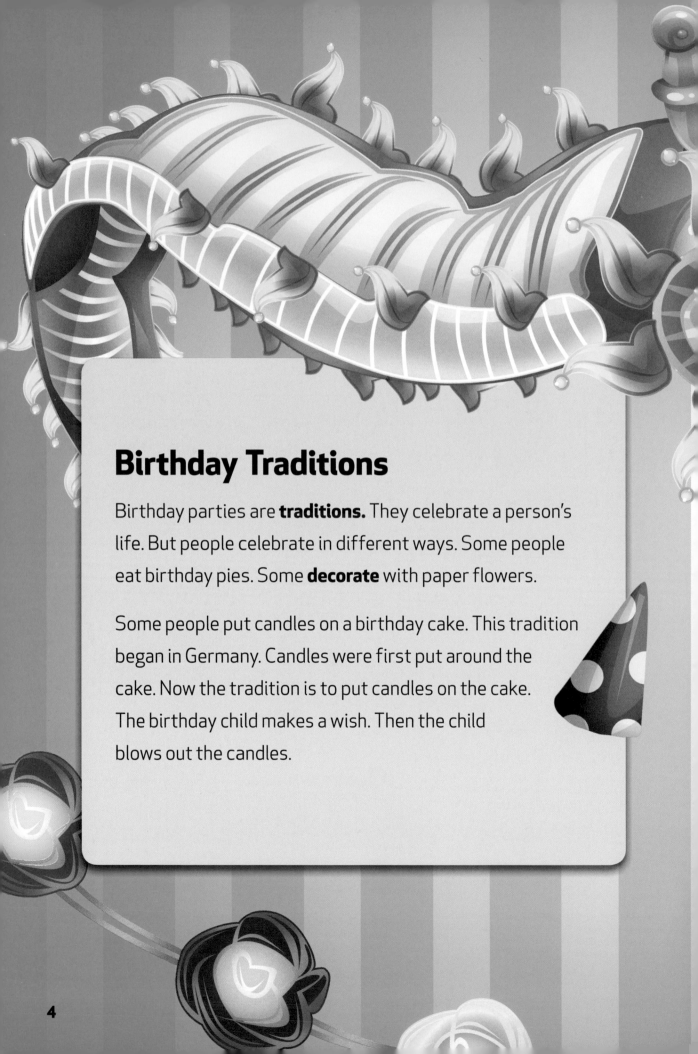

Birthday Traditions

Birthday parties are **traditions.** They celebrate a person's life. But people celebrate in different ways. Some people eat birthday pies. Some **decorate** with paper flowers.

Some people put candles on a birthday cake. This tradition began in Germany. Candles were first put around the cake. Now the tradition is to put candles on the cake. The birthday child makes a wish. Then the child blows out the candles.

These objects are used in different birthday traditions. Read to find out more about these and other objects from around the world.

North America

People in the United States have birthday traditions. People in Canada have similar traditions. A party room is decorated. Guests may bring gifts. They sing "Happy Birthday to You." The birthday child makes a wish. He or she blows out the candles. Then everyone eats cake.

Sometimes guests will receive party favors to thank them for coming.

Piñata

Piñatas are often part of birthday **celebrations** in Mexico. They are also used for other **occasions.** *Piñatas* are filled with treats. Guests hit the *piñata*. It breaks open. Then treats fall out.

South America

People in Brazil have flowers at birthday parties. The flowers can be paper or real. They eat chocolate bonbons. They also eat colorful candy.

Marzipan (almond and sugar paste) fruits and vegetables

Brigadeiros (chocolate bonbons)

Coxinha (shredded chicken and spices that are deep fried)

Birthday guests in Peru may get a *recordatorio* pin. The pins are decorated. People make them by hand.

The *fiesta de quince años* is a tradition. It happens in many Latin American countries. It is a **milestone** for girls turning fifteen. The birthday girl wears a fancy dress. She wears high-heeled shoes. She dances with her father.

Europe

Birthday cakes in England may hide small items. Tradition says the items show the future. A coin means a lot of money. A button means less money. A ring means marriage.

Some people in Switzerland plant a tree when their child is born. This is a tradition. They plant apple trees for boys. They plant pear trees for girls. They hope the child will grow as the tree grows.

Life candles are a German birthday tradition. The candle burns down one notch. The candle is lit every year until the child is 12.

Make Your Own Life Candle

What You Will Need
- 10-inch pillar candle
- Permanent marker
- Ruler
- Decorations

- Measure ¾ inch from the bottom of the candle and write 12.

- Measure and write numerals from 11 to 1 (from bottom to top). Each numeral should be ¾ inch apart.

- Decorate your candle with stars, stickers, sequins, glitter, and colorful shapes.

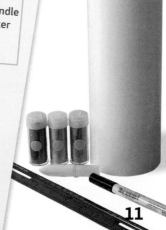

Africa

Some Egyptians have big birthday parties. They may even need two cakes! But they put candles on only one cake.

Children in Ghana have a birthday breakfast. It is called *oto* (AH-toh). It has eggs and sweet potatoes. Children eat fried plantains at parties. *Oto* and fried plantains are traditional foods.

Zulus do not invite guests to their birthday parties. Guests just show up. They eat, sing, and dance.

Asia

Chinese New Year is a special occasion. All birthdays are celebrated. All Chinese babies turn one year old then. This happens even if the baby is not a full year old.

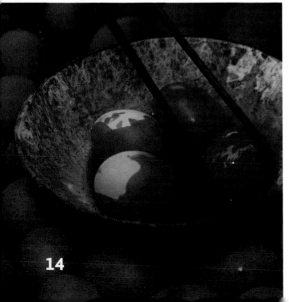

Eggs are dyed red for Chinese New Year.

People eat traditional long noodles at birthday parties. People eat them in many Asian **cultures.** The noodles **symbolize** long life. The tradition is to swallow them whole.

Shichi-go-san is a Japanese holiday. It honors girls turning three or seven. It honors boys turning three or five.

Oceania

Pusa at aso is a birthday party game. It is played in the Philippines. The "dog" protects its "bones." The "cats" try to take the bones away. The cats do not want to get tagged.

Pansit is a Filipino noodle dish. It can be made from long noodles.

People in Australia have a traditional party food. It is called hundreds-and-thousands bread. It is buttered bread with sprinkles.

Pass the Parcel is a party game. It is played in New Zealand. It is also played in other countries. Music starts. Players pass around a gift. It is wrapped in colored tissue paper. Smaller gifts are in layers of the paper. The music stops. The person with the parcel takes off a layer. The person keeps the gift.

New Traditions

Birthdays are fun occasions! Think about how other cultures celebrate. Then try a new tradition.

Check In   What makes a birthday celebration a tradition?

How to Make a Rainbow Cake

by Emily Brown

Birthday cake is often a big part of a **celebration**. Many cakes are chocolate or yellow. They often have chocolate or white frosting. The cake may be **decorated**. The frosting outside may look fancy. But the cake inside is plain.

Make your birthday cake fancy on the inside, too. Start a new **tradition**. Make a rainbow cake! The next pages have a recipe. You can use it with an adult. Make sure you have all of the **ingredients** first.

Ingredients

White cake mix

White cake frosting

Vegetable oil

Eggs

Food coloring

Directions

1 Follow the directions on the box of cake mix to make the cake **batter**.

2 Pour the cake batter into six small bowls.

3 Add red food coloring to the first bowl. Add blue to the second bowl. Add yellow to the third bowl.

4 Make three more colors in the remaining three bowls. Combine equal amounts of red and blue to make purple. Combine red and yellow to make orange. Combine yellow and blue to make green. Then mix the food coloring into the batter. Use a different spoon for each color.

5 Grease and flour a cake pan. Ask an adult to preheat the oven according to the directions on the box of cake mix.

6 Pour the first color of batter into the center of the pan. Slowly pour a different color on top of the first one. If you start with a dark color, use a light color next. Repeat for each color.

7 Have an adult bake the cake according to the instructions on the box of cake mix. Then frost the cake. Decorate it with sprinkles, candy, or whatever you wish.

Blow out the candles. Try a slice of cake.
Enjoy this special **occasion**. You are eating
every color of the rainbow!

Check In How is rainbow cake different from other birthday cake?

Discuss Text and Pictures

1. What do you think connects the two pieces that you read in this book? What makes you think that?

2. Choose a birthday tradition. Tell how the photos or pictures give you more information.

3. In "How to Make a Rainbow Cake," why is it important to follow the steps in order? How do the photos help?

4. What connections do you have to birthday celebrations? What questions do you still have after reading?